INTRODUCING

Kierkegaard

Dave Robinson and Oscar Zarate

Edited by Richard Appignanesi

ICON BOOKS UK   TOTEM BOOKS USA

Published in the UK in 2003
by Icon Books Ltd., Grange Road,
Duxford, Cambridge CB2 4QF
e-mail: info@iconbooks.co.uk
www.iconbooks.co.uk

Published in the USA in 2003
by Totem Books
Inquiries to: Icon Books Ltd.,
Grange Road, Duxford,
Cambridge CB2 4QF, UK

Sold in the UK, Europe, South Africa
and Asia by Faber and Faber Ltd.,
3 Queen Square, London WC1N 3AU
or their agents

Distributed to the trade in the USA by
National Book Network Inc.,
4720 Boston Way, Lanham,
Maryland 20706

Distributed in the UK, Europe,
South Africa and Asia by
Macmillan Distribution Ltd.,
Houndmills, Basingstoke RG21 6XS

Distributed in Canada by
Penguin Books Canada,
10 Alcorn Avenue, Suite 300,
Toronto, Ontario M4V 3B2

Published in Australia in 2003
by Allen & Unwin Pty. Ltd.,
PO Box 8500, 83 Alexander Street,
Crows Nest, NSW 2065

ISBN 1 84046 416 X

Printed and bound in the UK
by Biddles Ltd., Guildford and King's Lynn

A Radical Change in Philosophy

For over 2,000 years, philosophers had insisted that their primary task was to establish what counted as certain and reliable knowledge. Søren Kierkegaard violently disagreed. The job of philosophy wasn't to tell us what we could know. It had to tell us what we should *do*.

The Fork

Søren Kierkegaard was born on 5 May 1813, the youngest child of Michael Kierkegaard. His family nickname was "Fork" because, as a child, he had once threatened his dinner.

He was a frail child who suffered from a curvature of the spine, probably brought about by an earlier fall from a tree. He also suffered from mysterious fits that left him weak. And for the whole of his life he had an aversion to sunlight. Full-length portraits usually show him sporting an umbrella.

The Father

His old father was a remarkable man. He had been born in Jutland, as a landless serf, of an appallingly poor family.

He moved to Copenhagen at the age of 24 and rapidly became one of the most successful merchants in Denmark. By the age of 40, he was rich, so he retired from commerce and devoted the rest of his life to reading theology. He was a very intelligent and religious man – a great autodidact who enjoyed discussing Christian doctrine with the various churchmen he invited to his large town house.

The Paterfamilias

Michael Kierkegaard was also an authoritarian father who demanded correct behaviour and obedience from his seven children and was careful with his money. His religious views were a complicated mixture of orthodox Lutheranism, Moravian piety and an obsessive spiritual melancholy. It was a dark and grim Christianity that stressed the inevitability of sin, punishment and suffering. Søren had to learn a lengthy catechism and recite it to his father every day.

The Mother

Søren's parents were old when he was born. His "heavy minded" father was 56, and his mother Anne, 45. His mother had been the family's former domestic servant, illiterate, and she seems to have made little impression on any of her children. The father ruled, and was both feared and admired by all his children, especially Søren.

The Doomed Family

But out of the seven Kierkegaard children, only two survived. The young family and their mother were gradually obliterated by accidents, disease and complications of childbirth. Only Søren and his brother Peter remained. And their father thought he knew why. "The Great Earthquake" happened in 1835 when the old man told the truth at last. Søren was 22.

The Curse of God

God had rewarded Michael Kierkegaard with material prosperity, but was progressively punishing him by finishing off his children, all of whom would die before they reached the age of 34. (Like Christ, crucified at 33.) But why?

The Prophecy

He also confessed to pre-marital sexual relations with his second wife, while she was still a servant, which probably didn't please God much either. But it was his angry childhood blasphemy that had done for them all.

GUILT RESTS UPON THE WHOLE FAMILY. IT MUST DISAPPEAR, BE STRICKEN OUT BY GOD'S MIGHTY HAND. OUR REMEMBRANCE MUST BE CUT OFF FROM THE EARTH AND OUR NAME BLOTTED OUT.

Relief

Both boys seemed to have accepted their father's deranged explanation of the family's misfortune. They immediately became convinced that they would both die young. So 12 years later, Søren was very pleasantly surprised to find himself still alive.

Student Life

Søren became a student at the University of Copenhagen, studying theology and philosophy to become a pastor of the Lutheran church. But, perhaps because of doubts about his longevity, he gave up his studies halfway through. He moved out of his father's house, lived the life of a scandalous aesthete and devoted himself to a life of pleasure and amusement, which his father (surprisingly) seems to have funded.

The Holy Alliance

He soon discovered the joys of reading literature, as opposed to theology, and became an opera enthusiast. He caroused with several good friends who called themselves "The Holy Alliance". They discussed philosophy, girls and the opera, and Søren pretended to be more dissolute and outrageous than he actually was. By this time, he was developing more objective reservations about his father's extreme religious views, and even entertained serious doubts about his own Christian faith. And like most philosophy students then and now, he was worried about what to do with his life. Philosophy itself certainly didn't seem to have the answers.

Futility

The young Søren was a naturally serious individual, not really cut out for the life of a dissolute rake, even if he did his best. He ran up bills with booksellers, tobacconists and restaurants. He got drunk with his fellow students and maybe even had a sexual experience or two. But the life of pleasure soon came to seem forced and futile. He sank into a deep, almost suicidal despair at his lack of direction, and felt completely remote from the lives of his friends, who all found him wonderfully witty, if rather aloof.

Reconciliation

Fortunately, in May 1838, when he was 25, he seems to have had some kind of mystical experience that rekindled his religious enthusiasm. *"There is an indescribable joy which blazes in me."* He became reconciled with his now ailing father but, three months later, the old man died. This affected Søren deeply.

In his mind, returning to his father and God were more or less the same thing. He came to believe that his father had sacrificed himself so that his son could continue to preach God's message to the world.

Father and Son

Kierkegaard undoubtedly had some kind of complicated "father fixation". He projected the personality of his own very odd and stern father onto that of the authoritarian God he wrote about for the rest of his life.

He also seems to have inherited some of his father's mental instability. His religious frame of mind was equally obsessive, melancholic and guilt-ridden.

The Irony of Socrates

In 1840, after many years of interrupted study, Kierkegaard finally completed his degree in theology and was looking forward to becoming the pastor of a small country parish. He wrote a student thesis, "On the Concept of Irony, with Special Reference to Socrates". In this essay he praises Socrates for his attacks on conventional ideas and accepted wisdoms, and his impressive ironic detachment. Socrates mocks all those who are "fossilized in their limited social conditions".

I WAS ALREADY INDIRECTLY EXPRESSING MY OWN PERSONAL DISLIKE OF WELL-REGULATED SOCIETIES — COPENHAGEN IN PARTICULAR.

"Everything was perfect and complete and did not allow any sensible longing to remain unsatisfied. Everything was timed to the minute: You fell in love when you reached your 20th year, you went to bed at ten o'clock. You married, you lived in domesticity and maintained your position in the State. You had children."

Regine Olsen

By now Kierkegaard was in love with 18-year-old Regine Olsen. She was both pretty and intelligent, and he had admired her for some time. In September 1840, he proposed to her and was accepted.

A formal engagement of one year was agreed upon. So Kierkegaard was well on the way to becoming a highly respectable member of Copenhagen society, as his father would have wished.

A Dreadful Mistake

But the day after the engagement was announced, he knew he had made a dreadful mistake. He suspected that Regine had accepted him out of pity. Doubts and anxieties flooded into his mind. He was not husband material. His habit of deep thought and reflection made him "a lover with a wooden leg".

ANY GIRL FOOLISH ENOUGH TO AGREE TO MARRY ME WOULD SOON REGRET IT.

"Inwardly I saw that I had made a mistake. I should have to initiate her into things most terrible, my relationship with Father, his melancholy, the eternal darkness which broods in my innermost part, my excursions into lust and debauchery. The voice of Judgement said, 'Give her up.'"

The Broken Engagement

Kierkegaard panicked, broke the "very intellectual relationship" between them and returned Regine's ring in the following August of 1841.

Regine was reluctant to let him go, even though Kierkegaard insisted on telling her all the sordid details of his dissolute student days. He honourably pretended to be a corrupt "scoundrel" and "deceiver of women" so that people would think it was Regine and not he who had broken off the engagement. Copenhagen was a small, gossipy provincial city.

But Kierkegaard would not relent. *"So let us suppose I had married her. What then? About me there is something rather ghostly, which accounts for the fact that no one can put up with me. I was engaged to her for a year, and still she did not really know me. I was too heavy for her, and she was too light for me."*

Strange Deceiver

Regine finally gave him up and eventually became engaged to the rather more reliable Johan Frederik Schlegel, an earlier admirer. She remained puzzled and confused about the whole affair.

Escape to Berlin

Kierkegaard escaped from the Copenhagen gossip and a public scandal.

"I journeyed to Berlin. I suffered a great deal. I was so profoundly shaken that I understood perfectly well that I could not possibly succeed in taking the comfortable and secure middle way in which most people pass their lives. But it was she who made me a poet."

Finding a Way

In Berlin, he attended lectures by the Romantic philosopher **Friedrich Schelling** (1775–1854). As a determined bachelor, he spent the rest of his life praising the institution of marriage – from a distance. Regine became fictionalized in his mind as a kind of inaccessible muse. The whole sorry episode helped to make him into one of the most remarkable writers and philosophers of the 19th century. He had made up his mind what to do with his life, at last.

I SAT AND SMOKED MY CIGAR UNTIL I LAPSED INTO THOUGHT. YOU MUST DO SOMETHING. YOU MUST UNDERTAKE TO MAKE SOMETHING HARDER.

The Lectures

Schelling's lectures on the German philosopher **Georg Wilhelm Friedrich Hegel** (1770–1831) were also attended by other extraordinary radicals, among them the young **Karl Marx** (1818–83).The philosophy of Hegel was a powerful influence on all European intellectual life at that time.

What was Hegel's philosophy and why was it so influential?

The Hegelian Dialectic

Hegel believed that "Reason" is the best method of finding out the truth. But getting there was a complicated process. When you employ reason to investigate the world and its human inhabitants, you frequently end up with conclusions that seem utterly opposed.

This synthesis cancels out the superficial conflict between contradictions, preserves the element of truth in both and so helps advance the inevitable progress of human rational thought towards the "Absolute Truth".

Nevertheless, the process of "dialectic mediation" gets repeated throughout history, so that, in the end, human reason should be able to progress from lower levels of awareness until it reached the absolute truth about everything – human history, society, psychology, politics and religion. It was an evolutionary account of human knowledge and potential that appealed to many theologians, and even more to philosophers.

Objects and Thoughts

Hegelian dialectics is a logic of "ontology" (what is real) and idealist metaphysics (what is "really real"). It also dissolves the usually rather obvious distinctions that most people make between *real objects* in the world and *human thought*.

WHAT IS REAL IS RATIONAL; WHAT IS RATIONAL IS REAL.

Hegel argued that we need both *mental concepts* to categorize and explain the world of things as they appear to us, and *things* to give us something to think about. This means that "reality" must consist of both thoughts and objects, so the words "exist" and "real" take on rather odd all-inclusive meanings in Hegelian jargon.

Individuals and Communities

But it was Hegel's views on society and the individual that most exercised Kierkegaard. Hegel was impressed by how modern 19th-century civil society had progressed. The more society advanced, the greater was everyone's understanding and acceptance of individual rights and freedoms. But society had to be more than just a collection of individuals engaged in commercial dealings with each other.

The Individual Submerged

In Hegel's ideal society, the will of each individual and society's laws must coincide, because, ultimately, human beings are defined by their relation to others. That's why it was conceptually impossible to "resign" from society or claim that you were some kind of "outsider".

The conclusion of this Hegelian "system" is that the individual must be subordinated to the family unit, the family to society, and society to the State.

Kierkegaard's Criticism of Hegel

Kierkegaard was initially overwhelmed by the immensity and scope of Hegelian philosophy, but soon became disillusioned. Hegel's dialectic seemed to be a process of predetermined necessity in which individual choice was illusory or irrelevant. It was a world described from "outside" and had little to say to the young Kierkegaard trying to find out how to live.

THE ONE THING THAT HAS ALWAYS ESCAPED HEGEL IS — HOW TO LIVE. IT'S LIKE READING OUT OF A COOKBOOK TO A MAN WHO IS HUNGRY.

The Future and the Past

Kierkegaard's objections weren't just peculiar to his own personal situation. He went on to attack Hegel's "system" on purely philosophical grounds. He had a deep distrust of any philosophy that promised to be all-inclusive. Hegel's philosophy also seemed predominantly "backward looking". It had a "world historical" point of view but ignored how actual individuals live their lives – in the present, continually faced with decisions about their future.

Humanity Is Not an Idea

Hegel was simply too theoretical – obsessed by huge abstract concepts at the expense of particular real-life human beings who can never be reduced to mere concepts.

Philosophers had too long concentrated on the idea of "humanity" and ignored the fears, desires, thoughts, dispositions, neuroses and commitments of individual human beings.

Truth and Commitment

For Kierkegaard, discovering the "truth" is not just about finding out how things are. It's more a matter of making a commitment and taking specific kinds of action. Philosophy has to be more than just a calm search for objective truth.

IT HAS TO BE A PRACTICAL GUIDE TO LIVING, EVEN IF IT CANNOT TELL YOU EXACTLY WHAT TO DO.

Individual human beings constantly find themselves in a state of "paradox" (a crisis that needs to be resolved) and hope to find a "truth" (a resolution of the crisis, after making a commitment to a particular kind of action).

Fictional and Real People

Fictional characters in plays and novels are already provided with a "character" or "essence" that determines their destiny. With real people, the opposite is true. It is their *chosen actions* that cumulatively determine their character over time. In order to live and not aimlessly drift through life, you have to choose a specific "sphere of existence" – and that is always a gamble. It often requires immediate decisions and implies a commitment to act in certain kinds of ways in the future. Living is not an activity that can be "mediated" by some ongoing dialectic.

LIFE INVOLVES RISK. IT IS LIVED FORWARDS, INTO THE FUTURE.

So it is not possible to wait until afterwards and subject it to analysis and synthesis.

Is this Fair?

Kierkegaard's attack on Hegelianism has its attractions.

ANYONE WHO ONCE DESCRIBED HEGELIAN JARGON AS "TALKING WITH ONE'S MOUTH FULL OF HOT MUSH" GETS MY VOTE.

But Kierkegaard's criticisms are sometimes off the mark. Hegel openly admitted the inadequacies of his own philosophy. How could it possibly tell each individual how to live *a particular* life? Kierkegaard's own philosophy can sound dangerously "Hegelian" with its talk of "stages" and the attractions of the "universal". But the philosophies of Hegel and Kierkegaard seem wholly incommensurate. Kierkegaard's work is an "anti-philosophy" that rejects virtually the whole canon of Western philosophy with its emphasis on what is universal and objective, and on what can or cannot be known. Kierkegaard is playing a wholly different "language game" to Hegel. This makes it very difficult for anyone to analyze or criticize one in the terms employed by the other.

The Outsider

Kierkegaard returned to Copenhagen. He had finally come to realize that he was a natural "outsider" for whom the usual destinations of marriage and career were unavailable. Having rejected one specific way of life, he was naturally thinking about what it means to "choose" a specific way of life, and whether or not some forms of existence are superior to others.

IS LIFE SOMETHING THAT HAPPENS AUTOMATICALLY, OR IS IT SOMETHING ONE HAS CONSCIOUSLY TO **CHOOSE**?

The Philistines

Kierkegaard saw that most people were content to be absorbed into the everyday world of marriage, career and respectability. Most people follow the normal practices of their society. If the society is Christian, then they go to church. If it is communist, then they dutifully attend party meetings. That doesn't make them hypocrites, because they have probably never thought of questioning the social and economic pressures that govern their daily thoughts.

SUCH PEOPLE MAY OFTEN BECOME VERY SUCCESSFUL CITIZENS — BUT FOR ME, THEY AREN'T MATURE INDIVIDUALS.

"Everything must be reduced to the same level by producing a phantom, a monstrous abstraction, an all-embracing something that is nothing, a mirage, and that phantom is 'the public'."

The Crowd

The "crowd" have avoided all self-conscious reflections about the sort of life they lead. Kierkegaard mentions many examples of such "philistines".

They are contented members of the "public" but lack any real personal freedom, because they have allowed others to decide how they should live.

The Writer's Existence

Kierkegaard had chosen his own rather different way of life. He had made up his mind about his future at last.

I UNDERSTOOD PERFECTLY THAT I COULD NOT POSSIBLY SUCCEED IN TAKING THE COMFORTABLE AND SERENE MIDDLE WAY IN WHICH MOST PEOPLE PASS THEIR LIVES.

His father had left him a substantial legacy, which meant that he could become a full-time writer. His first real book *Either/Or* was published pseudonymously on 20 February 1843 and immediately became a literary sensation.

Either/Or

This book is a very odd mixture of puzzling prefaces, forewords, interludes, postscripts, appendices, letters, poems and diaries. There is no one declared "author" of the book but several. It is a wildly exuberant text, full of totally contrasting ideas about relationships, religion, marriage, seduction, metaphysics and art. Publishing under numerous pseudonyms became a habit for Kierkegaard, done partly to avoid yet more scandal. But he also wanted to create an "indirect" series of narratives told by different voices with different lives and opposed moral values.

Against Consensus

By wearing a series of fictional "masks", Kierkegaard could also speak out more clearly and dramatically, and let each character be wholly consistent in his views. What puzzled Kierkegaard's Danish readers was the lack of an overriding "authorial voice" in the book, one that finally steers the reader towards some sort of moral consensus.

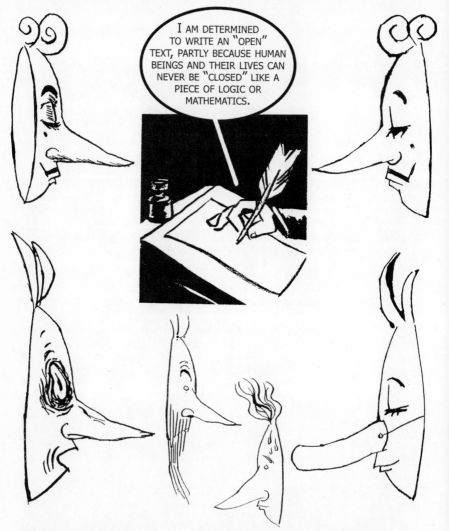

The lives of his characters are extreme, so there is no possibility of a Hegelian synthesis or reassuring "middle ground". That's why the book has its eccentric title *Either/Or* – because "Both-And" is the way to hell.

The Reader's Choice

Deciding upon which individual characters to admire and condemn is a more engaging exercise than arbitrating between abstract ideas. Some readers enjoy this disorientation process and the space it leaves for their own thoughts and opinions. Others like to be told what to think. But the choice remains resolutely either/or, not both/and, because this is what life is like.

Kierkegaard hoped that his book would help Regine to "push her boat from the shore". But he never forgot her and regretted never having a second chance to marry her. He wrote about her, indirectly, for the rest of his life, and finally left her everything in his will.

The Aesthete

Either/Or is edited by "Victor Eremita", a detached spectator of the world around him and a shrewd observer of his fellow human beings. He introduces us to a whole series of articles by "Aesthete A" about Mozart's opera *Don Giovanni*, modern and ancient tragedy, three fictional "betrayed women", a review of a comic play, a strange essay on "How to Defeat Boredom" and the extraordinary "Diary of a Seducer" written by someone called "Johannes".

EITHER/OR BEGINS BY EXAMINING WHAT IT MEANS TO LIVE THE LIFE OF AN AESTHETE, A LIFE DEVOTED EXCLUSIVELY TO SENSATION AND IMMEDIATE PLEASURES.

Don Juan

One of the main themes of the book is seduction. Don Juan – or Giovanni in Mozart's opera – is a spontaneous seducer of hundreds of women and has a "demonic zest for life". He has no moral principles and is indifferent to the suffering he causes to nearly everyone he encounters. He refuses to reflect on what he does, because, if he did, he would have to choose – to repent or carry on, but thereafter as a *consciously* unprincipled womanizer.

"Diary of a Seducer"

Johannes the Seducer is a more dubious character because he is reflective. He's well educated, intelligent and wholly aware that he has "a philosophy of life". *"I refuse to be bored and will devote myself solely to sensual pleasures."* He too is an outsider, which means he is not an unthinking "philistine". He is, however, a calculating rake who takes pleasure in the chase rather than the end result. His "Diary" tells us in great detail how he secretly investigates the weaknesses of his intended victim "Cordelia".

"We need no ring to remind us that we belong to one another. We drive into the sky through the clouds, the wind whistles around us. If you are giddy, my Cordelia, hold me close."

His poetic outpourings convince her and get her to the point where she virtually "seduces" herself. He sleeps with her and then immediately abandons her. He tries to persuade us of his good intentions.

He claims to be an "honourable" man, because he never promised to marry anyone, and never told lies. He appears to be self-deceived, not only alienated from the world and those around him, but also from himself.

The Aesthetic Life and Despair

The philistine is formed wholly by his social and economic environment, the aesthete by his natural instincts and feelings. But neither lifestyle is ultimately satisfactory. A life that is restricted to enjoyment and pleasure ends in despair, regardless of all the clever strategies the aesthete employs to fight off boredom.

The aesthetic life is, in the end, a series of repetitive experiences that gradually lose their allure, because every individual has a sense of the eternal which this sort of self-indulgent life can never satisfy. Time passes, and the young aesthete, "A", sees nothing more than duplication and death staring him in the face.

Emptiness

In a series of aphorisms in the section called "Diapsalmata" ("Musical Interludes"), this chosen way of life is revealed as empty and pointless, an endless dabbling with different art forms, people and careers.

Disillusionment

The Aesthete is extremely funny on the subject of "boredom". But because, unlike the vigorous Don Juan, he is a reflective intellectual, he is horrified by the egotistical nastiness of Johannes and able to examine what it means to live according to this self-centred world-view. He bitterly rejects the conventions of society that would force him into a dull marriage and onerous social conformity. But he is also very aware of the vanity of the temporal world – the source of all of his immediate short-lived pleasures.

Escape from Life

Very quickly, his way of life becomes more of an escape than a search. He drives out feelings of boredom and despair with short-term pleasures punctuated by long periods of lethargy and cynical pessimism.

So what is he to do? Rejoin the hordes of unreflecting philistines?

Judge Wilhelm

In part two of *Either/Or*, Judge Wilhelm appears with a vision of another "sphere of existence" for the despairing aesthete.

A life devoted merely to pleasure is doomed. Eventually the young man will run out of new sensations and his wealth and talents will fade away. Judge Wilhelm points out that "A" will always be unhappy because he will be forever trapped in reminiscing about past pleasures or hoping for new ones.

Marriage and Commitment

And that is when the "therapy" begins. The Judge says it is wrong to think of romantic love and social duties as inevitably opposed. There is much more to an ethical life than rote obedience to society's laws. In two letters to the young man, he argues that, although human beings are trapped in time, they can choose to develop and change.

Marriage brings with it a commitment to the future and changes one's conception of the eternal. This makes it an escape from the "immediate", as well as converting two individuals into active members of a stable community.

Choose Despair

Then the Judge gives the young man some rather odd advice. He tells him to "choose despair". By this, he means that a life devoted to disguising and escaping despair is futile. By *choosing* despair, the young man can face up to what causes his feelings of melancholy, recognize his guilt, repent, live by the superior categories of good and evil, and realize that life is more than just a game.

YOU WILL THEN ACHIEVE A MORE "TRANSPARENT" SELF, FREE OF HIDDEN FEARS AND REGRETS, ABLE TO ESCAPE FROM CLAUSTROPHOBIC SELF-INTEREST.

Judge Wilhelm also reassures him that the ethical life does not preclude an enjoyment of beauty and the good things in life – it is just that they are no longer the sole reason for living.

Ethics, the Individual and the Eternal

The good judge also insists that there is more to the ethical life than "crowd morality". *"Each individual must live life by choosing a set of moral principles and finding a place in the social order."* On occasion, ethical individuals may find themselves in conflict with the social norms of their community, but normally the ethical life brings contentment, because it gives meaning to the lives of those who choose it.

A "CIVIC LIFE" IS ONE OF MARRIAGE, CAREER AND SOCIAL RESPONSIBILITY.

THIS LIFE MAKES NO MENTION OF "SIN" OR "FAITH" ...

NEVERTHELESS, IT PREPARES ONE FOR AN EVEN HIGHER STAGE OF EXISTENCE — THE RELIGIOUS LIFE.

The ethical individual gains an overview of life, a greater sense of self, and changes his *conception of time*. Life is no longer merely a series of strategies to escape boredom and despair, but something related to the *eternal*.

Who is Judge Wilhelm?

Judge Wilhelm is, frankly, a bit of a bore, especially after the dubious thrills of Johannes the Seducer. Detailed accounts of sexual depravity are more fun to read about than ethical sermons. It doesn't help that Wilhelm is a very orthodox Protestant Lutheran, shares many of Michael Kierkegaard's opinions and, as his Christian name would suggest, has some rather Hegelian views.

The Judge's views on married life are also exceptionally rosy. Kierkegaard seems to have been partly fantasizing here about the life he might have had with Regine.

The Religious Life

Rather disturbingly, *Either/Or* ends not with some final words of advice from the wise Judge, but with a religious sermon from a simple country pastor.

Human beings are wilful, ignorant creatures trapped in time, and Judge Wilhelm's ethical life may be only a stepping stone to something higher and more mysterious.

Stages and Leaps

Kierkegaard returned to the notion of "Stages" or "Spheres of Existence" many times. Everyone is eventually faced with alternative ways of life – like bachelorhood or marriage. And each individual has to choose one or the other, because it is not possible to have "the best of both".

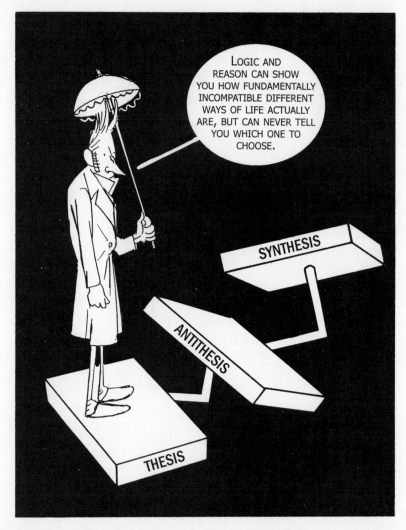

No "stage" is more "rational" than any other, so in the end every individual's choice is always "illogical". Everyone has to make a dramatic "leap" to another stage – usually because they are forced to do so by overwhelming psychological feelings of inadequacy and despair.

The Religious Stage

This kind of risk is especially true of the way of life that Kierkegaard aspired to – the religious world-view. The modern and deeply ascetic philosopher **Ludwig Wittgenstein** (1889–1951) agreed. Religion is a "form of life" in which the concepts and practices contained make sense only from "inside". No one can truly describe it for you.

Freedom is a Choice

For Hegel, human freedom is a derivative and collective idea – a concept that makes sense only within the ideals of the community. For Kierkegaard, "freedom" is a more absolute and mysterious human attribute that has meaning only when an individual **refuses** to submit to group approval.

It is exercising this freedom by *choosing* that makes you a true individual. *"In making a choice it is not so much a question of choosing the right, as of the energy, the earnestness and the pathos with which one chooses."*

What you choose is less important finally than how you choose. This is why Kierkegaard often presents his readers with highly persuasive exponents of wholly different sets of values, and leaves it up to each individual reader to decide.

THE AESTHETE'S DESPAIR MAY WELL LEAD HIM TO CHOOSE THE ETHICAL LIFE ...

THE ETHICAL CITIZEN MAY WELL EVENTUALLY JUMP INTO THE MORE DEMANDING RELIGIOUS LIFE.

BUT THE POINT REMAINS — EACH STAGE REQUIRES THE INDIVIDUAL TO "LEAP" FROM ONE TO THE NEXT.

There is no "Hegelian logic" of the inevitable about the climb upwards to "Absolute Truth".

Books, Books, Books ...

After the success of *Either/Or*, Kierkegaard produced a series of pseudonymous books at a phenomenal rate; although, by this time, most of Copenhagen's intelligentsia knew well enough who had written them.

FEAR AND TREMBLING,
JOHANNES DE SILENTIO,
1843

REPETITION,
CONSTANTIN CONSTANTIUS,
1843

PHILOSOPHICAL FRAGMENTS,
JOHANNES CLIMACUS,
1844

THE CONCEPT OF DREAD,
VIGILUS HAUFNIENSIS,
1844

STAGES ON LIFE'S WAY,
HILARIUS BOOKBINDER,
1845

CONCLUDING UNSCIENTIFIC POSTSCRIPT,
JOHANNES CLIMACUS,
1846

He also produced more orthodox signed works on religious themes, often published simultaneously with the more challenging works listed above: *Upbuilding Discourses* (1843–4), *Three Discourses on Imagined Occasions* (1845), *Upbuilding Discourses in Various Spirits* (1847), *Christian Discourses* (1848), *The Lily of the Field, The Bird of the Air* (1849).

The Swelling Mind

Kierkegaard's extraordinarily prolific output can be partly explained by his belief that he was condemned to die young. An equally convincing explanation for his incessant production line is that he was an obsessive thinker, determined to publish his ideas about virtually everything – philosophy, art, theology, human existence, and, perhaps most importantly of all, what it actually means to "become a Christian". It's an extraordinary record for someone who was physically rather frail.

The Imagined Future

Repetition develops an idea taken from the earlier *Either/Or*. It is impossible to classify either as philosophy or psychology but is a complicated mixture of both. Its fictional author is Constantin Constantius, a shrewd intellectual, who tells us all about a young man in love. A day or two after he gets engaged, an odd thought strikes him. He imagines his future, not as a happily married young husband but as a disillusioned old man, sunk in an armchair, remembering the love of his youth.

SO HE PANICS.

THE GIRL I LOVE IS THE MUSE WHO TURNED ME INTO A POET, BUT I'VE SEEN WHERE MARRYING HER MIGHT LEAD.

"She had made him a poet, and in so doing, she had signed her own death warrant …"

Indecision

The indecisive young poet breaks off the engagement. Constantius advises him to pretend to have a mistress. His outraged fiancée will go along with his plans – by rejecting him. He doesn't have the nerve to go that far, but, a few days later, wonders if he has made the wrong decision after all, and becomes an unhappy rememberer of "what might have been".

But then he reads in the paper that she has married someone else, so "repetition" is not possible. He commits suicide. Well, he does in the first version. By this time, Kierkegaard knew of Regine's engagement to another man, so he changed the ending. The young man now celebrates his independence as a writer.

"Being Present to Oneself"

Repetition is a curious tale of self-imposed misery, partly autobiographical and partly therapeutic. But it does explore further the idea of the self-deceived individual who drifts through life dreaming of an imaginary past and future.

> FOR YOUR CONTRIBUTION TO THE DEVELOPMENT OF THE COMIC STRIP ART.

> CLAP! CLAP!

> CLAP! CLAP!

> NOBEL PRIZE

> CLAP! CLAP!

> OR SOMETHING EVEN MORE COMPLICATED IN THIS STORY — SOMEONE IN THE PRESENT, THINKING ABOUT HIMSELF IN THE FUTURE, REMEMBERING HIS PAST!

It's easy to be nostalgic and believe that things were always better in the past. Or to hope that the future will be better than now. Both are common strategies that people use to avoid being "present to themselves". They end up indecisive, in a constant state of unspecific melancholy and regret.

Repetition is in the Present

So "repetition" can be a good thing – if it means a second chance to choose something you repent having lost. *Repetition* also reinforces the idea that it is best to live in the present, not in some imaginary elsewhere. And the "repetition" of marriage is one way of freeing yourself from imaginary hopes or sad regrets.

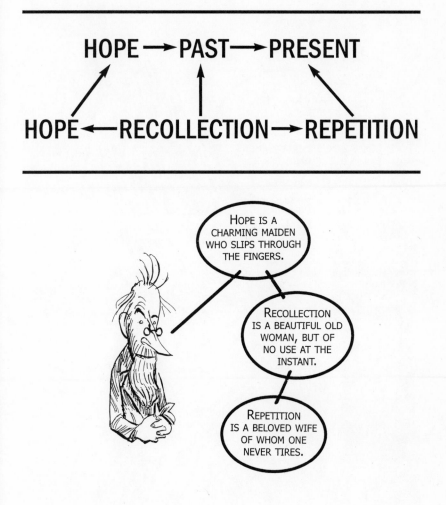

HOPE → PAST → PRESENT

HOPE ← RECOLLECTION → REPETITION

HOPE IS A CHARMING MAIDEN WHO SLIPS THROUGH THE FINGERS.

RECOLLECTION IS A BEAUTIFUL OLD WOMAN, BUT OF NO USE AT THE INSTANT.

REPETITION IS A BELOVED WIFE OF WHOM ONE NEVER TIRES.

What is Existence?

Kierkegaard claims that, until he finally decides what to do, the young poet does not really "exist". What does he mean? Clearly there's more to "existence" than just breathing, eating and thinking. The French philosopher **René Descartes** (1596–1650) was convinced he had proved that every thinking individual *has* to exist ("I think therefore I am").

THIS IS THE ONE CERTAIN PIECE OF SUBJECTIVE KNOWLEDGE FROM WHICH ALL SCIENTIFIC PHILOSOPHY IS ULTIMATELY DERIVED.

FOR ME, EVERYTHING "EXISTS" — PEOPLE, HISTORY, IDEAS, CONCEPTS AND "SPIRIT". IN MY "SYSTEM", DISTINGUISHING ONE FROM ANOTHER ISN'T EVEN THAT IMPORTANT.

BUT WHAT DOES HEGEL MEAN BY BEING? HE MAKES IT SOMETHING THAT NO HUMAN BEING EVER WAS OR CAN BE, A SORT OF PHANTOM.

Kierkegaard insisted that philosophical concepts and individual human beings "exist" in wholly different ways. The living, striving suffering self determines one's existence, not some remote abstract ego that is aware only of its thoughts.

Kierkegaard's point is a fairly elementary one. Concepts and reason can only ever tell us about the *possibilities* of existence, not about its actuality. A mathematician can happily use reason and concepts to tell us all about the possible areas and circumferences of a circular pond in the park. What he can't do is use reason to tell us whether or not such a pond actually exists.

No Guide to Choice

"Existence" is much more than just something you are born with. It is something you have to strive for, usually by distinguishing yourself from "the crowd", which may be biologically alive but doesn't "exist". This means that Kierkegaard's individuals are often asocial, or even anti-social, beings, at odds with those who surround them. Only by recognizing their true situation – knowing they are free to choose and consequently responsible for their choices – do they truly "exist" (or as later "existentialist" philosophers would say, do they become "authentic").

Dread, Despair and Guilt

This freedom to choose who you are, as well as what you do, sounds superficially rather attractive. But once you have made your decision, only you can be held responsible for it, if things go horribly wrong.

The choice of a way of life can be made only by the person who has to live it – which is what Kierkegaard means by his puzzling and famous phrase: *"Truth is Subjectivity."*

The Eccentric Dane

Kierkegaard himself had chosen a rather eccentric way of life. His days were remarkably uneventful. He rarely left Copenhagen; his whole life was one of writing, attending the theatre and taking brief journeys into the surrounding countryside.

On one occasion, I visited the farm where my father had worked as a shepherd boy.

He greatly enjoyed walking the streets of the city, a hunched figure in black, carrying his umbrella, talking to ordinary people, whose conversation he valued highly. Like most good Danes, he attended the State Lutheran church regularly, and now thought of himself as a "religious poet".

All of Kierkegaard's writings are, in one way or another, deeply concerned with the religious way of life. And, unsurprisingly, he disagreed violently with Hegel's analysis of religion and religious belief. Which takes us to his most important philosophical preoccupation – the relationship between religious *faith* and *reason*, a subject he wrote about extensively but again, pseudonymously, in his more "philosophical" works.

Beliefs and Uncertainty

Everyone has beliefs, from the everyday to the religious. Most of our beliefs are based on habit, some on reason and evidence, and rather a lot on faith.

A Faith Based on Reason?

For a belief to be "rational", some kind of proof or valid argument is usually presupposed. A belief based on faith, however, has more to do with a personal commitment, and usually appeals to some kind of transcendent authority.

OUR RELIGIOUS BELIEFS ARE AS DEMONSTRABLE AS ANY OF OUR OTHER BELIEFS.

NO. OUR BELIEFS HAVE MORE TO DO WITH AN ACCEPTANCE OF DIVINE AUTHORITY AND AN EXERCISE OF OUR OWN PERSONAL WILLPOWER.

Some philosophers and theologians suggest that reason and faith together can form solid foundations for religious belief. Others insist that the two are inherently incompatible.

Natural Theology

Those "apologetic" theologians who insist that reason and faith can be reconciled are sometimes called "natural theologians" or "compatibilists". They often argue that God's existence can be proved with reason. "Natural Theology" goes back at least as far as **Plato** (427–347 BC) and **Aristotle** (384–322 BC), who both appealed to transcendent entities like "The Good" and "The Unmoved Mover".

THIS EXPLAINS WHY, IN THE END, THINGS IN THE WORLD ARE AS THEY ARE.

GOD'S EXISTENCE CAN BE LOGICALLY DEMONSTRATED FROM HIS QUALITY OF PERFECTION.

THE WORLD SHOWS EVIDENCE OF DESIGN, SO THIS MUST PRESUPPOSE A DIVINE "DESIGNER".

PLATO

THEOLOGIAN **ST ANSELM** (1033–1109)   **ST THOMAS AQUINAS** (1225–74)

Rationalist philosophers – Descartes, **Gottfried Wilhelm Leibniz** (1646–1716) and others – also provided more elaborate versions of such "proofs".

Hegel's approach to this conflict between reason and faith was, essentially and typically, to *dissolve* it. For Hegel, God is not a transcendent being, but "immanent" – a part of all human beings and their spiritual selves. Indeed, God is identical with "Absolute Reality" – all that exists.

The mystery of the Incarnation – God becoming human in the form of Christ – is no more than an allegorical fable which tells us that divine and human natures are not radically or intrinsically different.

Religion and Philosophy

Religion merely hints through myths and symbols at fundamental truths, truths that philosophy ultimately reveals more clearly. Religion is imaginative and figurative; philosophy is rational and conceptual. Some theologians welcomed Hegel's "apologetic" explanation of the relevance and value of religion and agreed that it was a positive force for good.

RELIGIOUS BELIEFS REINFORCE THE UNDERLYING MORAL PRINCIPLES OF SOCIETY AND HELP BIND COMMUNITIES TOGETHER.

BUT PERHAPS THE COST OF HEGEL'S "MEDIATION" BETWEEN RELIGION AND PHILOSOPHY IS TOO HIGH ...

HEGEL HAS DISSOLVED CHRISTIAN DOCTRINE INTO VAGUE PHILOSOPHICAL MUSH.

Incompatibilists

One obvious problem for "compatibilists" is that Christianity's doctrines seem utterly beyond rational justification – God created the world from nothing; He is both one and three persons; and, as an infinite being, He took on a brief historical and finite existence in human form. Clever theologians can try to explain away these paradoxes. But a more radical way of dealing with them is to celebrate their very absurdity. After all, if God's existence could be *proved*, and Christian doctrine made logically demonstrable, then there would be no real need for faith in the first place.

Negative Theology

The Franciscan philosophers **John Duns Scotus** (1266–1308) and **William of Ockham** (1285–1349) were critical of all philosophical attempts to prove God's existence.

REASON CAN CLARIFY CONCEPTS, BUT TELLS YOU NOTHING ABOUT WHAT EXISTS OR DOESN'T.

THE FOUNDER OF PROTESTANTISM, **MARTIN LUTHER** (1483–1546), WAS EVEN MORE OF A "NEGATIVE THEOLOGIAN".

HUMAN REASON, IN HIS VIEW, WAS DEMONSTRABLY FOOLISH, LIMITED AND OF LITTLE RELEVANCE TO RELIGIOUS FAITH.

FAITH DOES NOT REQUIRE INFORMATION, KNOWLEDGE AND CERTAINTY, BUT A FREE SURRENDER TO GOD'S UNKNOWN GOODNESS.

Pascal's Wager

French mathematician and philosopher **Blaise Pascal** (1623–62) agreed that reason alone could not settle any matter of religious belief. He proposed a famous "wager". Belief in God is a better bet, because if you are wrong, the consequences are unknown to you; if you are right, heaven awaits.

The Ultimate Incompatibilist

Kierkegaard read and admired Tertullian, Luther and Pascal, as well as other, more contemporary theologians like **Friedrich Schleiermacher** (1768–1834), who argued that religion was its own "sphere of existence" which had nothing to do with reason. And Kierkegaard is himself probably the most radical and uncompromising incompatibilist of all time.

THE PROBLEM IS NOT TO UNDERSTAND CHRISTIANITY, BUT TO UNDERSTAND THAT IT CANNOT BE UNDERSTOOD.

Kierkegaard frequently insisted that his philosophy was always centred on one deceptively simple question. *"What is it to become a Christian?"*

State Christianity

For most people, becoming a Christian is mostly a matter of being born to Christian parents, observing certain religious rituals and getting warm feelings of solidarity and worthiness from church attendance. This was especially true of the Protestant Lutheran churchgoers in Denmark, who, as Danish citizens, were also required to be members of the State Church.

"Thus it was established by the State as a kind of eternal principle that every child is naturally born a Christian. The State delivers generation after generation, an assortment of Christians, each bearing the manufacturer's trademark of the State, with perfect accuracy, one Christian exactly like all the others with the greatest possible uniformity of a factory product."

Rational Christendom

Kierkegaard attacked what he called "Christendom". This included the majority of churchgoers in a secular and scientific age who declared that Christianity was a rational and sensible religion, based on true doctrines that Hegel had proven were the logical consequences of Western philosophical thought.

But, for Kierkegaard, becoming a Christian was a mysterious and agonizing process. No one really knew what it actually meant.

WE ARE ALL CHRISTIANS — WITHOUT HAVING SO MUCH AS A SUSPICION WHAT CHRISTIANITY IS ...

True Christians

Kierkegaard's Christianity is very different to this "Sunday Christianity". Every Christian is by definition an individual – so membership of some particular religious institution means very little. A true Christian is rarely happy or complacent. Kierkegaard's Christianity was like that of his father – a religion of guilt, anxiety and suffering. Christianity had to be a total way of life, which meant that it was impossible to be both a true Christian and a successful member of society. So absolute were its demands that the true Christian must necessarily be an "outsider".

Demonstrating Existence

"Attempts to prove God's existence are an excellent subject for a comedy of the highest lunacy." Kierkegaard makes the point time and again that it is impossible ever to *prove* that anything exists.

WHEN DESCARTES SAYS "I THINK", HE ALREADY PRESUPPOSES THE **EXISTENCE** OF A THINKER.

WHEN ST ANSELM CLAIMS THAT GOD HAS THE PROPERTY OF PERFECTION, HE ALREADY PRESUPPOSES THAT SUCH A DIVINE ENTITY **EXISTS.**

*"The entire demonstration always becomes an additional development of the consequences that flow from my having assumed that the object in question **already exists**. Thus I always reason from existence, not toward existence. I do not, for example, prove that a stone exists, but that some already existing thing is a stone."*

The Ontological Argument

Kierkegaard's criticism of the "ontological" argument is that you cannot drag the existence of *anything* out of definitions or some ingenious logic. However hard you try, God's existence cannot be proved like some kind of mathematical theorem. This is especially true for we finite beings whose intellects are exceedingly limited.

The Reasoning Irrationalist

A criticism that is often made about Kierkegaard is that he claims to despise philosophical method, is dismissive of reason, and yet uses both brilliantly in his attack on orthodox Christian "proofs" for God's existence. But Kierkegaard never says that being a Christian and using reason are incompatible, just that reason cannot make you into a believer. And, like Hegel, Kierkegaard rather celebrated the fact that it was a constant trait of rational thought to throw up irreconcilable paradoxes.

THE THINKER WITHOUT PARADOX IS LIKE A LOVER WITHOUT FEELINGS. THE SUPREME PARADOX OF ALL THOUGHT IS THE ATTEMPT TO DISCOVER SOMETHING THAT THOUGHT CANNOT THINK.

But, unlike Hegel, he never thought religious paradoxes could be "mediated".

Hans Lassen Martensen

One Danish theologian who professed Hegelian views was **Hans Lassen Martensen** (1808–84). He was a major figure in Copenhagen society, a frequent visitor to the Kierkegaard household and a reasonably tolerant and liberal cleric who tried to moderate some of Michael Kierkegaard's more pessimistic views about his vengeful God.

Believing in Christianity means accepting fundamentally absurd doctrines, especially those that define its founder.

Hegel's Christ

For Hegel, Christ's appearance on earth – the Incarnation – was a "pre-reflective" expression of the potential synthesis of the universal and particular, the finite and the infinite. The story of Christ, in other words, was a primitive kind of "picture thinking" that hinted at a deeper and more conceptual truth that later philosophers would clarify. Christ was no more than a concrete example of the conceptual unity attainable through the synthesis of apparently irreconcilable opposites.

The Folk Religion

The divine and the human can reach a dialectical synthesis because human beings have the "divine" in them. By being fully rational, the human mind gets close to the divine and so becomes Christ-like. Hegel therefore frowned on those Christians who believed in introspection, trusted their own individual consciences and worshipped a wholly transcendent God.

Kierkegaard's Christ

Kierkegaard argued both that the *object* of Christian faith is inherently paradoxical and that the *act* of Christian faith is itself absurd. There is a profound irrationality at the heart of Christianity that philosophy can never "absorb". The incarnation of Christ – the historical and finite existence of an infinite deity in human form – is utterly self-contradictory. It is logically impossible for the "temporal" and the "eternal" to co-exist.

THAT GOD HAS EXISTED IN HUMAN FORM, BEEN BORN, GROWN UP AND SO FORTH, IS SURELY THE ABSOLUTE PARADOX.

THIS PARTICULAR INDIVIDUAL HUMAN BEING – WHO LOOKED LIKE OTHER HUMAN BEINGS, TALKED LIKE THEM AND FOLLOWED THEIR CUSTOMS – WAS ... THE SON OF GOD!

And if God is a "transcendent" being, totally removed from the material world, how can Christ's existence on earth be explained?

The Transcendent God

For Kierkegaard, we are all pitiful and finite temporal beings whose understanding is woefully limited by our earthly situation. To think that we can ever have a God-like perspective, outside of space and time, is the height of folly. No one, not even Hegel, can reach a vantage point of "pure thought".

"As long as anyone exists, he is essentially an existing individual whose essential task is to concentrate upon inwardness in existing; while God is infinite and eternal."

Objective and Subjective Truth

Kierkegaard also challenged the long-held philosophical view about truth. The traditional philosophical conception of knowledge is one that downgrades individual truths, insists on going beyond a private point of view and looks at things dispassionately and disinterestedly. Kierkegaard despised this exclusive definition of truth.

IF SOMETHING IS TO BE **TRUE**, IT HAS TO BE **OBJECTIVE**.

IF TRUTH HAS TO BE TRUE FOR ALL, THEN IT IS NO MORE THAN A CONSENSUS OF GENERALIZED OPINION.

Everyone is aware of the fact that some emotional truths are subjective. I love my cat, but that's not a truth I expect anyone else to share. The indifference of others doesn't mean it isn't true – for me.

The same is true for the individual who has to make life-changing decisions that seem "true" for him or her. Very often these decisions have to be made at a particular moment, rapidly, in particular situations. There isn't a rule or guidebook to tell you what is "true for you". Kierkegaard frequently makes this point in exaggerated aphorisms like this …

"Our age is essentially one of understanding and reflection, without passion. Nowadays, not even a suicide kills himself in desperation. Before taking the step he deliberates so long and so carefully that he literally chokes with thought. He does not die with deliberation, but from deliberation."

The Leap of Faith

Another example of such subjectivity is religious "truths" for which the individual cannot get any external, rational warranty. This is obviously the case with a set of doctrines that are inherently paradoxical. *"When subjectivity is the truth, the truth becomes objectively a paradox; and the fact that the truth is objectively a paradox shows in turn that subjectivity is the truth."*

However ingenious his dialectic, Hegel cannot dispel the extraordinary contradictions lying at the heart of the Christian faith. True Christians must choose their own certainty – about an objective uncertainty – and enter a paradoxical state of mind that necessitates risk and a "leap of faith". So what is "faith"?

Faith is usually defined as a belief in something for which there isn't any proof or evidence. St Thomas Aquinas suggested that faith was for those without the intelligence or learning to follow his own complex philosophical "proofs". For Kierkegaard, faith is not some kind of second-rate belief, but a "passionate inwardness", the acceptance of a unique and precarious way of life. It has nothing to do with knowledge, proof or verification.

Faith and Proof

Christian faith is something that utterly transforms an individual's life, in the way that evidence, proof or knowledge never could. So, for example, if scientific evidence were found to show that matter can be made from "nothing", it would be interesting, but it wouldn't actually transform many people's lives. Faith is more like sight than knowledge – something immediate and vital – which means that to *prove* Christianity would actually make it emotionally vacuous.

A Way of Life

Faith involves a relationship with an invisible, eternal and transcendent God utterly remote from our temporal world, a relationship that often can produce feelings of guilt and despair in those committed to it (feelings that anyone outside of the religious life would just not understand). Kierkegaard's own brand of Christianity was a belief system that seemed to justify his own constant feelings of dread and guilt. He understood that perfectly well.

We can occasionally glimpse eternity in rare moments of personal revelation. But it has little in common with the orthodox Christian heaven – a total commitment to Christ's teachings in the past and his presence now – a whole way of life which abandoned all other "spheres of existence", even the ethical one. And that is what *Fear and Trembling* is primarily about.

Fear and Trembling

This book was published simultaneously with *Repetition* but is very different. *Fear and Trembling* is narrated by Johannes de Silentio, a man trying to come to terms with commitment to a religious way of life. His narrative centres on the biblical story of Abraham and Isaac. Abraham hears God's voice telling him to sacrifice his son on the top of the mountain; he obeys the command without question, and prepares to kill his first-born.

"Abraham built an altar there and bound Isaac his son, and laid him upon the altar. And Abraham stretched forth his hand and took the knife to slay his son."

The Divine Command

Fortunately, a sympathetic angel intervenes, and Isaac is saved. A "ram caught in a thicket by his horns" acts as a substitute. But Johannes remains shocked by the story. It seems such an unnatural, irrational and unethical act to even contemplate carrying out, and he finds it hard to accept the praise heaped upon Abraham's head for his obedience to God's command.

EITHER ABRAHAM WAS EVERY MINUTE A MURDERER OR WE ARE CONFRONTED BY A PARADOX WHICH IS HIGHER THAN ALL MEDIATION.

The Ethical and Religious Spheres

There is clearly a fundamental difference between the "ethical sphere" (as recommended by Judge Wilhelm in *Either/Or*) and this strange and disturbing "religious sphere" which seems to sanction infanticide. Kierkegaard was fond of taking stories from the Bible and re-examining them in this sort of way. And it *is* the tale of an imperious old patriarch and his more timid son, a story that appealed to Kierkegaard for rather obvious reasons.

The Religious Sphere

After a long struggle, Johannes comes to accept that, when a human being encounters God so directly, normal human ethics and codes of behaviour no longer apply.

FAITH IS PRECISELY THIS PARADOX, THAT THE INDIVIDUAL AS THE PARTICULAR IS HIGHER THAN THE UNIVERSAL.

Choosing total obedience to God's word requires a huge "leap" from the everyday world of traditional moral beliefs into a way of life that can make outrageous demands on the individual. In the end, Johannes recognizes the astonishing beauty of Abraham's faith, but is reduced to "fear and trembling" when he asks himself if he could do the same. He concludes that he personally is not ready to move on to this utterly incomprehensible way of life.

Beyond Civic Duties

Abraham's test is indeed a puzzling and disturbing story. Kierkegaard is deliberately overstating his case with this shocking example of how the religious life and the ethical life can be so far apart. The tale is also a veiled criticism of Hegel's plan to incorporate Christianity into the ethics of civic life. *"I for my part have applied considerable time to understanding Hegelian philosophy, and believe that I have understood it fairly well. Thinking about Abraham is another matter, however: then I am shattered."*

The Reader's Choice

The irrationality of Abraham's choice seems so absolute. It would be hard to imagine a greater crime than killing your own child. Most of us would maintain that his story of "voices" and his "reasons" were those of a madman. He could never justify his act to others. But the will of God, apparently, has little to do with the civic life of the community.

ABRAHAM'S DUTIES LIE NOT TO THE MORAL LAW BUT TO AN INCONCEIVABLY HIGHER AUTHORITY — THE WILL OF GOD ...

Perhaps it is best to think of Kierkegaard's story as a challenge. The reader must decide whether to excuse or condemn Abraham's obedience to divine command. Kierkegaard, as always, leaves the choice open. But his point is made: there is a huge difference between shared social norms and a system of values based on a wholly mysterious transcendent source.

The Knight of Faith

True believers like Abraham are essentially asocial. They will always come into conflict with the prevailing social norms of their society, whether these are Judaic, Roman Catholic, Communist or Lutheran. Kierkegaard certainly appears to commend what he calls "the teleological suspension of the ethical" – the claim that certain people like Abraham, a "knight of faith", are exempt from the moral considerations that the rest of us hold, even if he never says so directly.

BY HIS ACT HE TRANSGRESSES THE ETHICAL ALTOGETHER AND HAS A HIGHER CAUSE OUTSIDE IT ...

The French Existentialist philosopher **Jean-Paul Sartre** (1905–80), a great admirer of Kierkegaard, pointed out, rather dryly, that Abraham actually made two choices.

The Concept of Dread

The narrator of this odd book is Vigilus Haufniensis. He begins by remarking on the fact that "dread" (sometimes translated as "anxiety") is something that most philosophers have avoided examining. (Nowadays, of course, it is a subject examined almost to death by psychoanalysts.) The subtitle of the book is very strange – *A Simple Psychological Deliberation Directed Towards the Dogmatic Problem of Original Sin.*

THE BOOK WILL INVESTIGATE THE PROBLEM OF ANXIETY AS BOTH A PSYCHOLOGICAL AND A THEOLOGICAL ISSUE.

The Concept of Dread is a deeply autobiographical work that indirect narrative methods do little to disguise. Kierkegaard begins by drawing a distinction between "dread" and "fear". Fear is easy to explain.

FEAR IS A NATURAL HUMAN EMOTION WHEN AN INDIVIDUAL IS FACED WITH SOME KIND OF SPECIFIC DANGER.

BUT "DREAD" IS DIFFERENT ... A VAGUE FEELING OF MELANCHOLY AND UNEASE THAT NEVER SEEMS TO GO AWAY.

Dread or anxiety plagues certain individuals who are normally unable to specify the cause of it.

The Meaning of Dread

Dread is a symptom of "freedom's appearance before itself in possibility". Kierkegaard is saying that we are all free to choose *what* we do and so invent *who* we are. This is a fact most people are normally only half aware of, because they don't like to think about it too much. It's much easier to be a "philistine" member of the "public" and let others choose for you. But the knowledge of that fundamental freedom is always there, and the anxiety never quite goes away.

DREAD MAY BE LIKENED TO DIZZINESS. THE DIZZINESS OF FREEDOM WHICH OCCURS WHEN FREEDOM LOOKS DOWN ON ITS OWN POSSIBILITY.

Adam's Temptation

Kierkegaard clarifies the idea with a Biblical example. Everyone knows the story of Adam and Eve. Why did Adam break God's commandment and eat the apple from the Tree of Knowledge? The usual explanation is that the very prohibition tempted Adam and aroused his desire to break it. Kierkegaard's explanation is different. The prohibition awoke a dread of breaking it, which made Adam perpetually anxious.

THE PROHIBITION MADE HIM ANXIOUS, BECAUSE THE PROHIBITION AWAKENS THE POSSIBILITY OF FREEDOM IN HIM, THE ALARMING POSSIBILITY OF **DOING** IT.

Adam eats the fruit to free himself of his constant anxiety. God must have known that the temptation was immense. But, in the final analysis, the decision was Adam's alone and no one else's, so he has to take responsibility for it.

The Fear of Freedom

Kierkegaard's analysis of this "fear of freedom" is an intriguing one, pursued and expanded on by philosophers as different as Jean-Paul Sartre and **Erich Fromm** (1900–80). It can make individuals and whole societies "inauthentic". People, as individuals or en masse, are too often happy to "escape" this fear by retreating into an obedience to ideologies dictated by others.

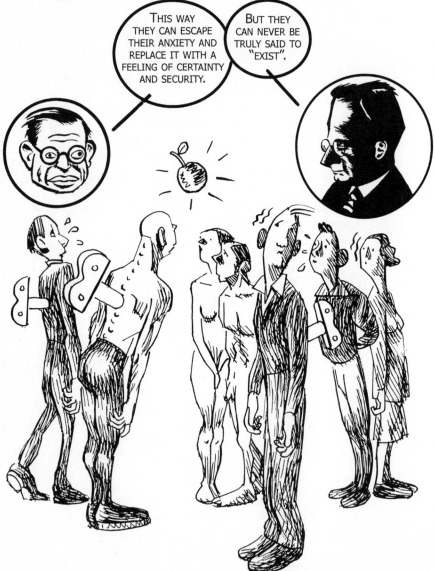

THIS WAY THEY CAN ESCAPE THEIR ANXIETY AND REPLACE IT WITH A FEELING OF CERTAINTY AND SECURITY.

BUT THEY CAN NEVER BE TRULY SAID TO "EXIST".

Inheriting Original Sin

The rest of *The Concept of Dread* contains odder ideas. Adam's "original" sin is inherited by everyone. Even worse, each subsequent generation adds on sins of their own, a millstone that grows larger and heavier from generation to generation as the human race progresses. Kierkegaard seems to have had rather Hegelian views about individuals and families in this regard.

So presumably, Michael's sin of blasphemy is one that his son also had to carry with him, to the grave.

Sex and Sin

Kierkegaard's views on human sexuality are also rather grim.

For Kierkegaard, this explains why thoughts of sexuality are always accompanied by feelings of anxiety. Sexuality is associated with Adam's original dread about breaking God's laws, the first sin and God's curse. There is something Manichean about Kierkegaard's depiction of his fellow human beings – as potentially pure spirits "trapped" in physical corruption. Kierkegaard undoubtedly had extreme anxieties about his own sexuality which he tried to escape by thinking of his own life as a progressive journey towards an ascetic life of "pure spirit". *The spirit has conquered so that the sexual is forgotten and remembered only in oblivion.*

The Age of Anxiety

Kierkegaard was the first philosopher to recognize that in our modern age many people experience feelings of "anxiety" for reasons not easy to comprehend.

Further Stages

Stages on Life's Way continues Kierkegaard's exploration of his own life and ideas about women, marriage, ethics, psychology, guilt and responsibility. Five fairly cynical male speakers discuss women and love and conclude that neither should be taken very seriously.

In one section of the book, "Guilty? Not Guilty?", "Frater Taciturnus" provides a detailed account of another year-long engagement that ended in disaster. All the complex feelings, thoughts and motives of the young man involved (called "Quidam") are analyzed and discussed in detail.

Like Kierkegaard, Quidam is obsessed by responsibility. If there is the remotest possibility of the marriage going wrong, then he should not commit to it. *"An ethical obligation cannot be cancelled out by the thought that it may not happen."*

The Nightmares

Quidam bravely attempts to examine the features and the causes of his unceasing melancholy. These are a complicated mixture of his own feelings of guilt and the depressive tendencies he inherited from his father – an old man who had the most horrible nightmares. Quidam, like Kierkegaard, shared a bedroom with his father, and at last begins to realize that the old man was a bit of a monster.

The book ends on a lighter note. Quidam ironically recognizes that life is suffering, and the way out of the swamp of personal despair is to make the leap into a third "stage" – the religious way of life.

The Sickness Unto Death

Kierkegaard thought *The Sickness Unto Death* was the best book he ever wrote, an opinion that not all of his readers now share. The theme is, again, despair – a state of mind most people are in for most of the time, even if they are not always consciously aware of it.

THERE IS NOT A SINGLE LIVING PERSON WHO IS NOT IN SOME DESPAIR, WHO STILL HAS NOT IN HIS INMOST BEING SOME DREAD OF THINGS UNKNOWN, A DREAD OF SOME POSSIBILITY OF LIFE, OR A DREAD OF HIMSELF.

Our Task of Therapy

Fortunately, the book tells us how to cope. As human beings, we are all given a unique individual self. For most people, this self is given by nature; but for a Christian, it is the product of a relationship to God. Feelings of despair are experienced by both, in different forms. Normally we assume that despair is a feeling that has a specific cause – like being abandoned by a lover.

As the human self progresses, it understands more about everything, including itself. But people who drift through life without recognizing the importance of this task will never become authentic human beings. Even a brilliant scholar, without this kind of self-awareness, can never become a successful human being, only some sort of brilliant analytical automaton.

THE MORE UNDERSTANDING INCREASES, THE MORE IT BECOMES A KIND OF **INHUMAN** UNDERSTANDING.

Willpower and the Self

The same is true of such other human attributes as sensitivity and the will. If your sensitive nature is directed at something impossibly large, like "all humanity", then it will become unreal and inhuman. "The Will" should also be exercised in immediate situations. The more "will" someone possesses, the more self is attained. But most people are without much willpower. They meander through life and avoid the challenging issue of *who* they are. Kierkegaard's views on will parallel those of several other 19th-century philosophers – in particular **Arthur Schopenhauer** (1788–1860) and **Friedrich Nietzsche** (1844–1900).

Neglect of the Self

Vague feelings of despair are an inevitable by-product of a "wilful" neglect of the self. For many, this is a deliberate strategy – to avoid the problem by ignoring it. For others, the avoidance strategy involves inventing some new self that they picture to themselves as a possibility never seriously achieved. Such individuals become "strangers" to themselves and on occasion become suicidal.

What is the Sickness?

For the "natural" man, death is tragic – the end of life. For a Christian, death is an event of less significance – merely one stage towards an eternal life. But for the committed Christian, these vague feelings of melancholy can turn into something much worse – *despair*, which is "sickness unto death". Paradoxically, the more one strives to be a good Christian, the more one becomes aware of one's own guilt, and its companion – a despairing sense of sin. The remedy is faith.

The Sickness Unto Death is the usual conflicting mixture of very incisive psychology and less immediately attractive Christian theology. "Being oneself" was not effortless – it involved a long struggle and a ruthless kind of honesty that most people would rather avoid. Kierkegaard felt he had to engage in this "self-struggle", and it destroyed what little happiness he might have achieved. He was always highly self-critical.

Being a True Christian

In one of his later books, *Training in Christianity* (1850), Kierkegaard declares that a true Christian had to be "contemporaneous" with Christ. Most 19th-century Danish citizens would be horrified if they ever chanced to meet Jesus – a carpenter's son accompanied by beggars and lunatics.

This doctrine completely dominated Kierkegaard in his final years, brought him ridicule and unhappiness, and outraged the State Church.

The Monastery in the World

After the broken engagement with Regine, Kierkegaard believed he had to choose between the life of the worldly aesthete or "the cloister". For a Danish Protestant, the monastic life wasn't really an option, so he spent his latter years as a recluse, reading theology and philosophy and writing his extraordinary books. Occasionally, he had "glimpses of the infinite", but he was never a fervent mystic or much of a radical dissenter.

I SAW MYSELF AS A PENITENT — EVEN IF MANY COPENHAGEN CITIZENS DISAGREED.

HE'S THAT IMMORAL WRITER WHO WROTE SCANDALOUS BOOKS ABOUT THE SEDUCTION OF YOUNG WOMEN.

The Applicant Pastor

Denmark was an absolutist monarchy with Protestant Lutheranism as its official State religion, and Kierkegaard still retained thoughts of becoming a Lutheran pastor in a small country parish. Bishop Mynster, the old family friend who had debated theology with his father, thought that Kierkegaard's own religion was "pitched too high" for him ever to be a humble country preacher – a judgement that now seems rather astute. Kierkegaard was rather too keen on self-denial, suffering and hellfire to suit most rural parishioners.

WHEN I ASKED HIM IF THERE MIGHT BE A FREE PARISH I COULD GO TO, THE BISHOP REPLIED ...

WHY DON'T YOU FOUND ONE OF YOUR OWN?

Kierkegaard finally gave up all thoughts of being a church employee and branded the Christianity of Denmark as "Christendom" – a worldly, hierarchical and authoritative institution devoid of any true spirituality.

CHRISTENDOM, IN WHICH A NICE, GRUNTING, PROSPEROUS BOURGEOIS, PROVIDED THAT HE IS GENEROUS TO THE PASTOR, IS SUPPOSED TO BE THE EARNEST CHRISTIAN.

The Church was a "machine that just kept buzzing on". If it were proved that Christ never actually existed, he said, how many good Christian churchmen would actually resign their posts?

The Wild and the Tame

Kierkegaard also wrote a series of fables in the manner of his old "Holy Alliance" friend, **Hans Christian Andersen** (1805–75), about the early Christian church, comparing it to the corrupt and tame institution that now went under its name.

A TAME GOOSE CAN NEVER BECOME A WILD GOOSE. BUT ON THE OTHER HAND, A WILD GOOSE CAN WELL BECOME A TAME GOOSE. SO – BEWARE!

IT IS MY FATE TO BE TRAMPLED TO DEATH BY GEESE …

Bishop Mynster

Kierkegaard hoped that Bishop Mynster would reply publicly to the criticisms of the State Church in *Training in Christianity*. But the bishop died in late January 1854. Denmark's most famous theologian, Professor Martensen, in a funeral eulogy, called the bishop a "witness to the Truth" – a man good enough to be one of the original apostles. Kierkegaard was outraged. Mynster had been a comfortable careerist, not exactly a man called on to justify his faith, and, worse, far too tolerant and liberal for Kierkegaard's austere religious tastes.

The Instant

Kierkegaard felt deceived by Mynster, a man he had once admired. Mynster was no true apostle: he had hardly suffered the agonies of the soul, or been mocked and martyred like the early disciples. Kierkegaard's views became more shrill and extreme, published in a broadsheet that he himself produced – *The Instant*.

Nine issues were produced, between May and October 1855. On occasion, Kierkegaard seems to have been attacking the very man he himself might have become. *"The priest is snugly settled in his rural residence, and with a prospect, also, of attractive promotion; his wife is plumpness itself, and his children no less."*

The *Corsair* Incident

A few years earlier, Kierkegaard had been embroiled in a witch hunt against him that was partly of his own making. *The Corsair* was a flippant satirical paper with a very large circulation that specialized in mocking and debunking the rich and famous in Copenhagen. An old friend of Kierkegaard, P.L. Moller (perhaps the original model for "Johannes the Seducer"), wrote a mocking review of *Stages*, criticizing the character "Quidam" and identifying him clearly with Kierkegaard himself. Putting young women through some kind of experimental mental torture, he wrote, was despicable.

IF YOU WISH TO REGARD LIFE AS A DISSECTING ROOM, AND YOURSELF AS A CORPSE, VERY WELL.

BUT TO WEAVE ANOTHER PERSON INTO ONE'S SPIDER'S WEB, DISSECT HER ALIVE, OR TORTURE THE SOUL OUT OF HER, LITTLE BY LITTLE, IN THE NAME OF EXPERIMENT — THAT IS NOT PERMISSIBLE.

Kierkegaard was understandably outraged by the review and, unwisely, wrote a rather pompous reply defending his book. *The Corsair* went on the attack. Kierkegaard apparently only pretended to support the poor, when he was himself ridiculously wealthy. Cartoon images of him appeared every week, exaggerating his thin legs, ridiculous trousers, stove pipe hat and stooped walk. Once he had enjoyed his daily walks, talking with ordinary people. Now they pointed at him and yelled out derisive names.

It was an episode from which he never fully recovered. He became more of a recluse, more of a political reactionary, and even more critical of the popular press, which reduced individuals to an unthinking mass of anonymous hostile faces – "the public".

"The Present Age"

In his essay "The Present Age", Kierkegaard reflected on the whole sorry episode. The modern age was one in which people were curious about everything but committed to nothing – thanks to the new popular press flooding them with unsifted information. All meaningful differences became erased.

The Modern Public

In this modern age, everybody has an opinion, usually not their own, based on information that is anonymous and derivative. The new phenomenon of "the public" is born.

A PUBLIC IS NEITHER A NATION, NOR A GENERATION, NOR A COMMUNITY, NOR A SOCIETY, NOTHING CONCRETE, NO REAL COMMITMENT.

The "crowd" is a mass of spectators, fighting off boredom, unable to distinguish between the important and the superficial. They make second-hand, risk-free pronouncements about ideas and the lives of others, and have no true opinions of their own. What Kierkegaard would have made of our own tabloid press, TV soaps and the Internet doesn't require much guesswork.

Last Years

By 1848, at the age of only 35, Kierkegaard looked and behaved like an old man. His reduced economic circumstances meant that he had to sell the family home and move to an apartment – though he still enjoyed good wine and maintained two servants. He continued to write huge amounts, and produced several "edifying discourses" on the Christian faith. He still believed in his mission to restore the Danish State Church to an earlier, purer state.

I HAVE A CONSTANT FEELING THAT THERE IS SOMETHING HIGHER STIRRING WITHIN ME. WHAT MUST BE EMPHASIZED IS THE FOLLOWING OF CHRIST.

Major political events such as the European uprisings of 1848, the war with Germany and the end of Denmark's absolute monarchy seem to have passed the misanthropic writer by unnoticed. Regine's father died in 1849, and Kierkegaard wrote her many letters, which her husband wisely returned.

Kierkegaard qualified his admission by insisting that the purpose of his unacknowledged works was always to arouse feelings of religious yearning in his readers.

Sickness and Death

The Editor of *The Corsair*, Aaron Goldschmidt, was actually an admirer of Kierkegaard's earlier work and rather regretted his lampooning of the now isolated and vulnerable writer.

IT WAS TIME FOR HIM TO DIE, FOR POPULARITY WAS THE LAST THING HE COULD ENDURE.

On 2 October 1855, Kierkegaard collapsed in the street and was taken to Frederick's Hospital.

The Deathbed

Both of his legs were paralyzed and some disease seemed to be taking over his whole body. He refused to take Holy Communion, even from his old friend, Pastor Emil Boesen.

He died on 11 November 1855 and was buried at the family lot. His nephew and self-appointed disciple, Henrik Lund, protested at the orthodox Lutheran service conducted at the graveside. Today, Kierkegaard's memorial slab leans over precariously, but is prevented from falling to the ground by the pedestal of his father's more impressive monument.

The Legacy

No one today would deny the massive influence Kierkegaard has had on the recent history of philosophy, psychology, theology and other varieties of human thought. Kierkegaard himself would probably have been distressed to find himself and his work championed by atheist existentialists, humanist theologians and various postmodernists and deconstructionists. But he really has only himself to blame.

Kierkegaard the Aesthete

Kierkegaard's numerous "Socratic" debates often make for an exciting and challenging read. They can also be frustrating for those who would like a more lucid and coherent exposition of Kierkegaard's own views. But that is to misunderstand Kierkegaard's whole project. He was determined that his work would give readers space for their own thoughts and self-discovery.

IT MAKES THE READER HIMSELF ACTIVE — THE OPPOSITE OF THE MODERN METHOD OF LEARNING, LIKE A PARROT.

Kierkegaard floods us with possibilities and questions, not doctrines. This can be a dangerous strategy. Kierkegaard might be critical of the aesthete's lifestyle, but no one has better anatomized its characteristics with such perception, imagination and sympathy as he did. Those who read Johannes' "Diary of a Seducer" are apt themselves to be seduced!

The Production Line

Kierkegaard is not a conventional or systematic philosopher. He has no one clear thesis backed up by coherent argument. He was a compulsive scribbler who wrote a vast amount, in the form of published philosophical works (mostly under assumed names), letters, newspaper articles, dissertations, journals, religious discourses, explanations of his authorship, religious fables, and those final diatribes against clerics and magazine editors. He was a psychologist, novelist, autobiographer, theologian, arts critic and poet, as well as a philosopher. He established a different kind of philosophical writing especially suited to his own beliefs …

IT IS THE SPECIFIC INDIVIDUAL WHO MUST BE THE FOCUS OF ATTENTION AND NOT SOME GENERAL ABSTRACTION LIKE "HUMAN NATURE".

HE ESTABLISHED A TRADITION OF THE "PHILOSOPHER-NOVELIST" THAT MANY EXISTENTIALIST WRITERS HAVE ADHERED TO.

THIS MEANS EXAMINING PHILOSOPHICAL ISSUES IN THE ACTUAL CONDITIONS OF INDIVIDUAL EXISTENCE.

Kierkegaard was very "modern" in this respect, even if some of his views about sexuality, politics and society now seem rather "Victorian".

How to Approach Kierkegaard

Sometimes Kierkegaard's work is treated as if it is little more than a continuous and rather exhaustive dialogue with other philosophers – especially Hegel. This approach can make Kierkegaard's work seem no more than a critical commentary – which isn't the case. Sometimes his writings are probed by amateur and professional psychoanalysts for information about his inner psyche …

Case studies of the miserable Dane can make for a fascinating read, but there is still rather more to Kierkegaard than a neurotic bundle of sexual repression, hypochondria, father-fixation and religious mania.

The Father of Existentialism?

Kierkegaard resisted encapsulation into any kind of "movement" or academic philosophy. His own work received little attention for many years after his death, until recognized by 20th-century existentialist philosophers, **Karl Jaspers** (1883–1969), **Martin Heidegger** (1889–1976) and Sartre.

Who is an Existentialist?

Perhaps it should come as no surprise that Existentialist philosophers disagree as much as they agree – if Existentialism is indeed "the philosophy of the individual".

But all of them were hostile towards much of the "Western Philosophical Tradition" with its focus on the abstract problems of knowledge.

The Anonymous Crowd

Kierkegaard witnessed the emergence of a modern world that swallowed up individuals to produce the "monstrous abstraction" of "the crowd" and "the masses". His contempt for "the public" was founded partly on his own timidity and sense of difference, but also from his rejection of the Hegelian notion of the individual as a mere component of the family, community, society and the State.

THIS AGE HAS FORSAKEN THE INDIVIDUAL IN ORDER TO TAKE REFUGE IN THE COLLECTIVE IDEA.

THIS REJECTION OF CONVENTION AND THE "RESCUE" OF THE INDIVIDUAL BECAME CENTRAL TO ALL EXISTENTIALIST PHILOSOPHIES.

Indifference to Choice

Western philosophy had too long encouraged "understanding and reflection without passion", a cold, disinterested detachment from real life. Philosophers, in Kierkegaard's view, were self-deluded academics imagining they had reached some "Absolute Truth" that removed suffering from life and invalidated personal choice.

PHILOSOPHY HAD TO BE "ENGAGED" AGAIN WITH THE IMMEDIATE FUTURE OF INDIVIDUALS TRYING TO DECIDE WHAT TO DO WITH THEIR LIVES.

PEOPLE ARE CONSTANTLY FACED WITH "EITHER/OR" DILEMMAS. TO BE TOLD THAT THEY ARE A SMALL PART OF SOME "COLLECTIVE SPIRITUAL SELF-REALIZATION" ISN'T OF MUCH USE.

THE WAY OF OBJECTIVE REFLECTION MAKES THE SUBJECT ACCIDENTAL, AND THEREBY TRANSFORMS EXISTENCE INTO SOMETHING INDIFFERENT, SOMETHING VANISHING.

The Objectively Subjective

For Kierkegaard, the most fundamental truths that affect real people aren't "objective" at all. The "truths" about our specific human relationships in our everyday dealings with each other and society, our belief in God, are matters of passion and commitment in which "reason" and "knowledge" have only a very small part to play.

Passionate Belief

It is the passion and intensity of our beliefs that determine their "truth", not some kind of external verification. And this is especially true for all of those religious beliefs that are intrinsically unprovable.

Existence and Human Presence

Kierkegaard's central theme is existence. Not the existence of objects and ideas, but human beings. He continued to ask what it meant to "exist" as a human being. He was obsessed by the fact that we all exist in time, and not for very long. This makes the whole idea of our "existence" rather urgent. You can stroll through life avoiding any thoughts at all about such problems, and yet survive perfectly well by copying what everyone else does. That's what most people do, after all. But you won't "exist" – not as an individual.

Or you can live the life of a detached observer trapped in a world of abstractions and systems.

But truly to exist, you have to face some fundamental truths about "the human condition" and decide what your response is going to be.

Responsibility and Commitment

Another central existential truth (or doctrine) is that every individual is free. We all constantly have to make choices about what to do with our lives. These choices will, obviously enough, accumulate and ultimately determine the sort of human being we eventually become. Kierkegaard envisaged this process as a series of dramatic choices between "stages" or "spheres" – those that he had himself contemplated choosing at different times.

Only we can choose *what* we do and decide *who* we are. We have to demonstrate our "ownership" of these key decisions by showing our commitment to them.

Cowardice

Many people develop strategies to avoid crucial decision-making and commitment.

The responsibility that comes with making irreversible decisions is arduous. If things go wrong, other people may get hurt, you may ruin your whole life, and if any of this happens, then only you are to blame. This unpleasant truth is often expressed psychologically in vague, unspecific feelings of unease that are simply an inescapable part of truly "existing". Kierkegaard thought that this "angst" might also have deeper theological roots to do with every Christian's feelings of sin and guilt which only God could remove.

Existentialist Key Words

No modern existentialist would now share Kierkegaard's rather bizarre views on accumulative original sin. But nearly all of them agree with the rest of his diagnosis. Kierkegaard invented most of the conceptual key words of existentialism.

What Does He Mean?

But is Kierkegaard's own brand of existentialism convincing? It's often difficult to criticize Kierkegaard because he uses these special key words in his own unique, and sometimes rather slippery, way.

HIS READERS CAN SOMETIMES FEEL THEY ARE BEING LED INTO A MAZE WITH NO APPARENT EXIT ...

I USE WORDS TO MEAN WHAT I WANT THEM TO MEAN.

He also celebrates paradox and absurdity when they stimulate the need for religious faith, and yet is quick enough to spot and criticize illogicality elsewhere.

Subjective Truth

Kierkegaard's verbal gymnastics are best exemplified by his central doctrine of "subjective truth". Most philosophers since Plato have required some kind of objective proof or evidence for something to be "true".

Being critical of all closed "systems" does not justify Kierkegaard's own extreme inconsistency. Even his famous "stages" are sometimes two, sometimes three, and sometimes five. And he's not always clear how they interrelate or don't.

Are We Really "Free"?

All existentialist philosophers are non- or anti-determinists. They have to be, if they want to stress the value of human freedom. This makes "freedom" mostly an ethical or "value" word. An act that is freely chosen is morally superior to one that isn't. Making free decisions is what marks you off from "the crowd", even if this then subjects you to a battery of unpleasant feelings like despair and anxiety. And so on.

BUT ARE WE AS FREE AS KIERKEGAARD INSISTS WE ARE?

Existentialist philosophy tends to evade or disguise the complicated *empirical* issue of free will by appealing to each individual's "feelings" of freedom. We are free, because, well, it **feels** that way.

The Issue of Determinism

But the ugly supposition of determinism may not be so easy to avoid. Kierkegaard was always hostile to the "human sciences" because they examine human beings abstractly en masse and lose sight of what makes each individual most distinctive. But other philosophers, psychologists and geneticists would resolutely question how free we are to make "our" own decisions so that we can truly "exist".

Is the Mind Transparent?

Many Existentialists, including Kierkegaard, also tend to go along with the Cartesian model of the mind – that, when it comes to choosing, the mind is "transparent" and open to inspection by its owner. But many psychologists have shown that we are only dimly aware of the mental processes that go on in our heads. If this is so, we may be forced into "choosing" certain kinds of beliefs and actions that are only very superficially "ours". **Sigmund Freud** (1856–1939) would have some interesting things to say about Kierkegaard's endless feelings of guilt and sin.

The Uncertainty of Freedom

Kierkegaard's dreadful childhood clearly had *some* determining influence over his whole life.

Social Products

Existentialism is a very "Romantic" philosophy in its celebration of the individual and condemnation of the "crowd". But the brutal fact remains that we are all inescapably social animals, products of our cultural environment, shoved around by economic forces that probably do determine our "consciousness" as much as Marx claimed they do. It may be comforting to believe in our own particular uniqueness, but we remain complicated products of our social and cultural environment, in ways that are not always personally clear to us.

MY OWN UNIQUE LIFE AS AN AESTHETE, SCHOLAR AND RELIGIOUS ENTHUSIAST WAS, AFTER ALL, ONLY MADE POSSIBLE BY THE HUGE PROFITS FROM MY FATHER'S GROCERY BUSINESS.

The Abstraction of Freedom

Marx would have criticized Kierkegaard for the sin of "abstraction" – treating "freedom" and "religion" as transcendent truths when they are not. Kierkegaard's own fixation on a pure or "absolute" individual freedom often seems like an "abstraction".

HE SAYS ALMOST NOTHING ABOUT THE SORT OF SOCIETY THAT WOULD HAVE TO EXIST FOR MORE THAN JUST A FEW FORTUNATE INDIVIDUALS TO BE "FREE" TO CHOOSE.

Most people are limited by political, social and economic conditions that severely restrict the range of possibilities open to them. So Hegel may be right to insist that words like "freedom" need to be defined with some precision.

We may not be absolutely free to choose who we become. Perhaps we **should** still behave as if we were "free" in spite of all this determinist baggage. But then, it isn't always clear if the "freedom" Kierkegaard talks about is a fact or a value – or more puzzlingly, something in between. And are all those "philistines" quite as bad as Kierkegaard thinks they are?

Kierkegaard's Grandchildren

Without Kierkegaard's conceptual framework for examining the human condition, the philosophies of Heidegger and Sartre would have been inconceivable. Heidegger followed Kierkegaard in agreeing that it was indeed a special form of "existence" that marked human beings out from everything else in the world. How and what we choose will determine who we are. But Heidegger is more aware of the limits placed upon us that are not of our own making.

Heidegger popularized the term "inauthentic" that became a hallmark of Existentialism.

Sartre's existentialism begins with the premise that there is no God and that the Universe is therefore "absurd". If there is no divine authority to fall back on, then this places an even greater emphasis on the roles of human freedom, choice and responsibility.

Sartre provides a thorough account of the various strategies people of "bad faith" use to avoid having to face the grim reality of choice.

Modern Theology

There is good reason to make Kierkegaard the first modern theologian. Being a "Christian" is a life commitment to one's personal relationship with God, not just passive obedience to a set of conventional rules and doctrines. All subsequent "existentialist" theologians have shared this view – although not all of them would agree that the more paradoxical a religion is, the more faith it requires, and so the more admirable it becomes.

But when we believe something, it seems more of an involuntary process in which conscious decision-making is absent. We do not consciously "will" oranges to be orange or 2+2 to equal 4, for example. But Kierkegaard is surely right to stress how belief is intimately connected to an individual's dispositions, actions and whole way of life.

Existentialist Theologians

Few modern theologians are so determinedly focused as Kierkegaard was on suffering, sin, guilt and fear as the only convincing verification of a true Christian. Karl Jaspers thought that Kierkegaard's Christianity was too negative.

IT ADMITS OF NO MARRIAGE, NO OFFICE IN THIS WORLD, AND NOT MUCH ENJOYMENT OF ORDINARY EVERYDAY EXISTENCE EITHER.

KIERKEGAARD WAS TOO ISOLATED FROM THE COMMUNAL NATURE OF RELIGIOUS FAITH AND THE ROLE OF "GOOD WORKS" IN CHRISTIAN LIFE.

KARL BARTH
(1886–1968)

BUT HIS FOCUS ON THE CONTRAST BETWEEN TEMPORAL HUMAN EXISTENCE AND DIVINE ETERNITY HAS TO BE A CRUCIAL ASPECT OF THE CHRISTIAN FAITH.

RELIGIOUS FAITH HAS TO BE SEEN AS THE "GROUND OF BEING".

PAUL TILLICH
(1886–1965)

Perhaps Tillich comes closest to Kierkegaard's stress on the crucial role of choice in Christian life, the immense gulf that exists between human beings and a limitless God, and the paradoxical nature of much Christian belief.

Postmodern Anti-Philosopher

Kierkegaard is praised today for being in line with the tradition of "anti-philosophers" which began with Socrates and currently ends with "postmodern" philosophy. Kierkegaard distrusted essentialist metaphysics. Logical concepts can tell you nothing about really important subjects – such as how to lead your life. Kierkegaard seems a typically postmodern anti-essentialist.

Is There a "True Self"?

Kierkegaard was also prophetically "postmodern" in his distrust of monolithic objective "truths" and his refutation of the Enlightenment faith in dictatorial "reason". Most postmodernist philosophers, however, would now have deep reservations about his insistence that "subjectivity" must be the core definition of what makes us human.

Adorno, Irigaray, Derrida

In spite of such reservations, many contemporary philosophers – the Marxist **Theodor Adorno** (1903–69), radical feminist **Luce Irigaray** (b. 1932) and deconstructionist **Jacques Derrida** (b. 1930) – have all written books on Kierkegaard.

Derrida has deconstructed the Abraham–Isaac story, this time by claiming that Abraham's "gift" of his son to God somehow established a more equitable relation between God and Abraham.

The Open Reading

Kierkegaard always maintained that he was an "author without authority". He is our postmodern contemporary by recognizing that authorial meaning is "deferred", "ironic" or "dialogic" – never permanently stable and never "closed".

The way he organized language was as important to him as what he had to say – another reason why reading Kierkegaard is always worthwhile. Most of us will read Kierkegaard for his extraordinary ideas and insights. Kierkegaard will continue to be read long after books like this one have disappeared.

Further Reading

Kierkegaard wrote 35 books, mostly between 1842 and 1850, and also filled 22 volumes of his extraordinary *Journals.*

Virtually all of Kierkegaard's work is now available in English translation, notably in the *Collected Works of Kierkegaard*, translated and edited by Howard and Edna Hong (Princeton University Press).

More readily accessible are the Penguin editions of an abridged *Either/Or* (1992), *Fear and Trembling* (1985) and *The Sickness Unto Death* (1989), all translated and annotated by Alastair Hannay. *Either/Or* is the book to read first. It's a stimulating and enjoyable introduction to the strange world of Kierkegaard.

Books on Kierkegaard's life and works include:

📖 *Kierkegaard*, by Walter Lowrie (Oxford University Press, 1938), was the standard biography but is now out of date.
📖 *Kierkegaard*, by Patrick Gardiner (Oxford University Press, 1988), gives a thorough account of the life and is good on the philosophical background to much of Kierkegaard's work.
📖 *Kierkegaard*, by Alastair Hannay (The Arguments of The Philosophers series, Routledge, 1982), is excellent, but perhaps difficult for those with no philosophical education.
📖 *The Cambridge Companion to Kierkegaard*, edited by Alastair Hannay and Gordon D. Marino (Cambridge University Press, 1998), contains some useful essays.

Some more general books on modern European thought that examine Kierkegaard's work in the context of other philosophies include:

📖 *From Rationalism to Existentialism*, by Robert C. Solomon (Harvester Press, 1978; Rowman & Littlefield Publisher, 2001).
📖 *An Introduction to Modern European Philosophy*, edited by Jenny Teichman and Graham White (Macmillan, 1998).

Two books that concentrate on Kierkegaard as radical theologian are:

📖 *Kierkegaard*, by Julia Watkin (Outstanding Christian Thinkers series, Chapman, 1997; Continuum, 2001).
📖 *Subjectivity and Paradox*, by J. Heywood Thomas (Blackwell, 1957).

Readers with an interest in the philosophy of religion might enjoy the hefty three volumes of *Nineteenth Century Religious Thought in the West*, edited by Ninian Smart et al. (Cambridge University Press, 1988), and *Reason and Religious Belief*, edited by Michael Peterson et al. (Oxford University Press Inc., 1998).

The most accessible book on the philosophy of Kierkegaard's arch-enemy remains Peter Singer's *Hegel* (Past Masters series, Oxford University Press, 1983; Oxford Paperbacks, 2001). *Heidegger* by Richard Polt (UCL Press, 1999) is – remarkably, considering its subject – both thorough and accessible. Sartre's own *Existentialism and Humanism*, translated by Philip Mairet (Methuen, 1977) is very readable – as, of course, are all of Sartre's novels published by Penguin and others. (See *Nausea*, and the trilogy: *Iron in the Soul*, *The Age of Reason* and *The Reprieve*. Sartre's autobiography *Words* is also published by Penguin.)

Two books mentioned at the end of this one are Theodor Adorno's *Kierkegaard: Construction of the Aesthetic*, translated by Robert Hullot-Kentor (University of Minnesota Press, 1989), and Jacques Derrida's *The Gift of Death*, translated by David Wills (University of Chicago Press, 1996), which plays both interesting and occasionally tedious deconstructive games with the ideas of "gift", "obligation" and "death".

And finally, David Lodge's *Therapy* (Penguin, 1996) is an amusing and moving novel about a successful but unhappy man who studies the works of Kierkegaard and finds them therapeutic.

About the Author and Artist

Dave Robinson has taught philosophy to students for many years. He is also the author of several Icon books – *Introducing Descartes*, *Introducing Ethics*, *Introducing Philosophy*, *Introducing Rousseau* and *Introducing Russell*.

Oscar Zarate has illustrated many books in this series, including *Introducing Freud*, *Introducing Melanie Klein* and *Introducing Psychoanalysis*.

Acknowledgements

The author is, as always, indebted to his Stakhanovite editor, Richard Appignanesi, whose own book *Introducing Existentialism* (Icon Books, 2001) is highly recommended. He is grateful to Oscar Zarate for his enthusiasm, sense of humour and friendship, and because he is an amazingly inventive illustrator. And he is thankful that he took that irrational leap from dissolute bachelorhood into marriage with his partner Judith, and not *just* because she is his unpaid proof-reader.

Index